Fragments and Found Things

Fragments and Found Things

Poems by

Theresa Rogers

© 2025 Theresa Rogers. All rights reserved.
This material may not be reproduced in any form, published,
reprinted, recorded, performed, broadcast,
rewritten, or redistributed without
the explicit permission of Theresa Rogers.
All such actions are strictly prohibited by law.

Cover design by Shay Culligan
Cover image by Christopher Laurence Tierney
Author photo by Theresa Rogers

ISBN: 978-1-63980-992-9
Library of Congress Control Number: 2025949663

Kelsay Books
502 South 1040 East, A-119
American Fork, Utah 84003
Kelsaybooks.com

*to Shaun
and to Christopher*

Acknowledgments

Thanks to the editors of the following publications where earlier versions these poems first appeared:

Cape Cod Poetry Review: "Wellfleet"
Cape Cod Times Poetry Page: "Descanso"
Cathexis Northwest: "thirty-three"
English Bay Review: "Last Fall in Coal Harbour"
San Diego Reader: "I once read," "memory care"
Sheila-Na-Gig: "Ode to the Tri-State Area"
Uppagus: "In midwinter," "Bark"
Vancouver Poet Laureate City Poems: "the stone artist"

Contents

I once read   15

I

A doll and a swing   19
In midwinter   20
Summer dunes circa 1964   21
Bark   22
Harold "Papa Flash" Edgerton, Whitney Museum 2018   23
Ode to the Tri-State Area   24

II

Is it *not* a bed   27
Leaving me in Dún Laoghaire   28
Telling me about Aurelia   29
memory care   31
A daughter's writ   32
Elegy from my balcony   33

III

Wellfleet   37
September at Long Pond   39
the stone artist   40
Still life in a black and white   42
Hunger   43
Last Fall in Coal Harbour   44

IV

prehistory   47
Descanso   49
thirty-three   50
cauldron   51
Late June swim   52

V

lost: a found poem   55

*. . . so many things seem filled with the intent
to be lost . . .*

—Elizabeth Bishop

I once read

a person misplaces
up to nine objects a day—
painted clay ashtrays
cherry red hula hoops
china dolls and diamond
rings—

    a father at six.

By 60 we have lost
two hundred
thousand
things.

I

A doll and a swing

You watched as I swayed
in the backyard swing
cradling my yellow-haired
cloth and plastic doll
offering, with my spare hand,
a blue-helved metal spoon
to its tiny split-cherry mouth

You wondered how little
could be asked or needed—
only this and the soft nectar
of honeysuckle bines tangled
in the jungle gym nestled
in the nearby sandbox

I learned later of your witness—
a trace of tears on downy skin
reflected in the bay window,
your sad question to my mother,
your daughter—*is she all right?*

Perhaps I was humming a song,
a lullaby of my own to soothe
the slack doll—needing little
and asking even less

In midwinter

for N.

the ice buckled under us.   We dropped

as one   into that black pool.   In those days

our two girlhoods were still thick

as warm chocolate milk.   Somehow we crawled out; we grew.

You stopped fondling my small breasts.   You let them fix

your freckled nose.   We hadn't drowned.

     We made it home.

You raised three daughters of your own; I raised sons.

     We drop as one.

Summer dunes circa 1964

Here at the end of the fire road tunneled with pitch pines the mist unwraps the edge of the sandspit near the dune I once slid down with a pack of cousins collecting grit in our pants while listening to the adults on the beach crack oyster shells harvested from shallows while drinking martinis and telling jokes we didn't understand though the timbre of their laughter would reach deep into evenings cool enough for blankets at the drive-in where we ate hot dogs and oily popcorn while sitting in plaid nylon chairs watching Betty Boop dance on a screen extending into a universe where we didn't think to ask why it was never like this at home.

Bark

we ran feral in loamy woods
shooting arrows and guns

you played father for me
high in the rough bent
arms of the cherry tree
marking the thin margin
between our homes

by twelve you had already grown
into the man they had carved

>I looked for you
through windows
around doorjambs
as the heroin leaked
into leaden pipes

I was your *wild thing*

>you sculpted my guitar
from boards,
nails & rubber bands

Harold "Papa Flash" Edgerton, Whitney Museum 2018

Atomic Bomb Exploding

We pause at the shot
of the slow-motion bomb

forming a smoke crater
shaped like a child's skull

perched on an elongated
iron neck still wired

to the ground.

Nearby someone whispers:

> *should Truman have been tried*
> *for war crimes?*

***

As small children
we clasped our fingers

around bowed heads
and folded under

wooden desks, each
air raid siren piercing

our tiny eardrums

Ode to the Tri-State Area

I want to swing under a branch
       of that liberty apple tree
swim through blue-green algae
       and snap back at turtles
I want to collect bullfrogs to mate
       in giant dill pickle jars
before freeing the tadpoles and
       the glinting fireflies too
I want to make toys of wooden
       spools and rubber-bands
in my stepfather's workshop
       and play in the deep woods
with boys before they learn
       to lunge all sweat and tongue
I want to Hula-hoop in the driveway
       with my best friend and fill up
our bike tires and ride to Caldor's
       to pocket gum and lip gloss
I want a mirror vanity for my room
       Scotch-taped poems on the walls
to climb up the rusted water tower
       and scan life beyond this town
I want to drink from a fat white
       coffee mug rich with Coffee mate
take the Metro line to the City and learn
       to drive to Jones Beach in the Chevy
and away from the house where I still
       smell honeysuckle from my window

II

Is it *not* a bed

of roses?

It feels like one—
fleshy petals of childhood,
a complacent lull

that soon veers left
into a gnashing, rushing
bloody mess—

Stems begin to entwine
bits of disappointment
shedding curled leaves
of promise after loss/
loss after promise

And the bed?
Tossed site of de-flowering fury—
life resides there

Leaving me in Dún Laoghaire

       you and I fell in that ruined
city of evenings so slow

they pushed back into afternoons

       bitters and lime stuck
to our tongues until I was alone

in the pitch of your tin whistle

       too high for someone raining
down as your morning savior

       —no, survivor—

       you would vow to marry another
woman from this same brown

       city, one who
would beat her bodhrán for you—

Telling me about Aurelia

At your wedding
under a white tent
in late hot summer
in the Midwest
we celebrated

you were so assured
until she left—
and you wept for hours
in my two-room walkup
on Thompson as Larry Bird
soared across polished maple

and after *The Deer Hunter*
on Christmas Eve you didn't
want to be alone so we carried
home a spindly city pine
hoisting it five flights up
the dark bent staircase

you slept on my couch
for months or a year

and now you tell me—
she raised your son alone

and with the screech and slide
of subway cars still ringing
in her skull she walked
across her cold and golden
Indiana field strewn

with salt brown shards
of broken whiskey bottles
and dried corn husks
to lay herself down

memory care

you took your leave
from us in slow breaths
each exhale measured
against the last

and the next

I sat
for a while
in the garden
where they grew
squash and borage
for the old ones
as a kind of prayer
to moldering flesh—
and to the slow abandon
of this cache of attachments
to memory, to care

and yes I'm sure I heard

only barely

as you whispered our names

A daughter's writ

I summon your sneakers carefully cut away
            to release bunions and bent toes

I summon your scores of spent leather purses
            full of small change I once pilfered

I summon your gimcrack jewelry and mothballed
            ski sweaters in cardinal red and cobalt blue

            I wear forever on my back

I summon your collection of embossed silver stolen
            from your ever unlocked house

I summon your little red car jammed with bicycle pumps,
            inner tubes, the stuff of escape—

            tell me, where are they now?

Elegy from my balcony

It starts   with a brace of wild   geese
crossing my balcony   their fierce wings   flapping through
thin clouds—

         a crease of orange light   that only evening brings
to the seams   of water and sky   marking the end
                       of every spent day.

This is when I think of you.
         It takes this raucous flock
             so fiercely free to bring you
back again   reclaiming me over
             and over as yours   each wing-
beat a new wound, the roar
         of the rush past.   Until across
     the sound   one by one   here
and there   dangle serried lights   like dancing paper dolls
freshly torn   and tucked back in   to the night.

III

Wellfleet

At the flea market, a watercolorist points
to a tiny splash in her picture of a cottage
on a dune by the sea.
She says one night
a hundred people stood on the dune watching for whales
and three came by and spouted.
And just then all those people quietly joined hands.

I don't know, she says,
*the whales and the sense that we are all connected to something
   larger . . .
it wasn't long after 9/11.
Anyway, you can see one of the whales
breaching in my picture.
I just put in one
but if you look at it long enough
the other two will appear.*

A painter was late to her studio
one day last year because
of the wild turkey in a mating dance
outside her plate glass window.
*The male sashayed around the hen
for nearly three hours.
He came closer and farther like this,*
she says, *gracefully swirling her hands.
For hours. Can you see?*

A sculptor crafts mobiles out of wood
and stones and starfish and nuts,
making these alternate universes
because, she says, *I don't like the one I'm in.*

I ask three fishermen on the beach,
who are there all day,

how can you be so patient?

September at Long Pond

Women congregate like gulls
in black bathing suits
legs in water, arms folded
speaking of their days
as their lined faces
deep with abundance
soften in the falling sun
muting the creases

I sit on the wooden bench
As my brother-in-law reads
Virgil's first Eclogue
of forsaken kids laid to die
in the shadow of a rock
of the expelled goat herder
who is offered sweet apples
cheese and soft chestnuts

And meanwhile children here
dig soft tunnels and moats
in sand now theirs to recast
before it tenses into the cold

the stone artist

is tending to his cairn
again, gently balancing

one jagged stone
on to another

until each is poised
impossibly on its own

thick sea rock pressing
into mussel shells

bruised and broken

each day brings
a new topology

along the curved seawall
of the far Northwest

lined with silver trees—
cavenio sagrada (Españoles)

or cascaras to those
who first paid witness

still, his sculpted birds

won't wing or birth
as they keep vigil

in cold winds
and king tide swells

asking only
for one last moon

before starting their slow
slide back to the sea

Still life in a black and white

The way he stands
rolled jeans, hips slanted
beat-like next to a Chevy,
dust black and steel-toothed—

his plaid checked shirt tucked
in like his enigmatic smile.

His right arm traces down
to casually grip her fingertips.

Her chubby legs jut out
below the white-laced pinafore.

Her other hand frames a tiny
twisted grimace; her thin
shadow bends and hides
under white-walled tires.

Her left foot raised

                    as if poised to flee.

Hunger

a boy slouches on the street against

      the damp wall of a liquor store

his tattooed fingers rest lightly

      on his sleeping dog's greasy collar

a woman drops small coins

      that ping into his steel-riveted cap

a boy slouches on the street against

      a wall with a dog and some coins

Last Fall in Coal Harbour

This evening the seawall speaks
in tongues as the granite-haired man
plays Moon River on his sax.
Small dogs are leashed to women
wearing black spiked heels.

Tide presses docks squealing
and straining against the steel
girding them to the stone bank:

> *what if the shore became the sea*
> *and the sea our walkways?*

Floatplanes groan across the inlet
on swollen pontoons lifting
over the crowded cruise ships
heading out to the inside passage —
foghorns rending deep into the port.

Holding his painting close
to his cheek, the sidewalk artist says
finally and plainly to passersby:

> *in the end you choose between*
> *the movement and the details.*

IV

prehistory

    the small boy sits in the sun

      spending time being   becoming

innocent of strata of compressed earth below:

                     fractured and riven by heat, pressure, water

the untidy accumulation of extinct lifeforms

    dwelling in and out of time scales

                 in overlapping waves

of contours and cleavages

             visible only in brief moments—

if only I could see directly

       through his blue-green eyes, translucent skin, slight bones

                 nothing (of him) would be wasted

                 less would be lost

Offspring

for C.

He says

Australia is way past Jupiter
and tomorrow is only the next day—
that infinity is everywhere
added to eleven
and
        when it is very quiet
                he hears the earth spin.

He tells me

he is my *night and shiny armer*
the sweet of my dreams—
that I should say
only the good words
and
        when we are really still
                we feel the earth spin.

Descanso

for S.

and so they tie a board
to the fence, a leash fastened with a marker

invites short elegies: *ocean brother*
shred in   ride forever te amamos (we love you)

strewn goldenrods and pepperbush dry slowly
near bottles of Blue Moon, two rubber sandals—

>vestiges of original agreements
>once sworn as if on vellum

I watch the surf carry you and your brother
deep into the ocean to slide over swells
curling into your own glassed waves

>and I know this collision
>of grief, fragments and found things

>if you have other pulls to summer
>they are slight

thirty-three

as a child in Catholic school
I was made to pray

in church I slid off the pew
to the kneeling board
to repent as I was told

a fat Bishop slapped my face
to welcome me   I didn't believe

then you left in your Jesus year

it was not the blue hour or gold
but deep night when you walked
out into the world

to leave it   and us   behind

I would get on my knees
now and every day
not to pray   but as a beggar

I might even be humbled
by the gift of pink streaks
across my cheek

cauldron

losing one
too precious
to live

without

takes me down
to the bent bones
of my knees

Grief is ancient
the sage says to me

Persephone rises
from the underworld

torn from the privilege
of unknowing

as the Earth
grieves its loneliness

the universe
its vastness

Late June swim

I lift my head to look past
the dock—where two white
wooden chairs sit in waiting—

and up to the lean of fragile pines
with fascicles thick and green
against the blue

I hear my lungs rattle
as each stroke strikes and
cleaves the soft pond

I want to escape grief's bones,
its breath—swimming is
my new religion

tomorrow, this.

V

lost: a found poem

from "Fi" by Alexandra Fuller

you can give your child anything—
you can give him life

until it is lost

his beautiful body with its rhythms and tides,
its breath, heart, and spinal fluid—

if I could figure out where he's gone

I would follow him there

About the Author

Theresa Rogers is a poet and teacher who splits her time between Vancouver, Canada and Wellfleet, Massachusetts. She grew up with her mother and sisters in several small towns in Westchester County, New York where she was able to play freely in backyards, roam the woods, and skate across frozen lakes.

She has published poems in *The English Bay Review, Cape Cod Poetry Review, Uppagus, Cathexis Northwest, San Diego Review, Sheila-Na-Gig,* and the *Cape Cod Times* Poetry Page. She won second prize, emerging poets, in the Vancouver City Poems contest. She received an MFA in poetry from Antioch, Los Angeles, and is professor emeritus at the University of British Columbia. She currently serves on the board of *poetry in canada* and as poetry editor for the *Cape Cod Review.*

Website:
theresarogerspoet.com

www.ingramcontent.com/pod-product-compliance
Lightning Source LLC
Chambersburg PA
CBHW030916170426

43193CB00009BA/866